Original title:
Hearts Rebuilt

Copyright © 2024 Swan Charm
All rights reserved.

Author: Swan Charm
ISBN HARDBACK: 978-9916-79-120-2
ISBN PAPERBACK: 978-9916-79-121-9
ISBN EBOOK: 978-9916-79-122-6

Whispers of Renewal

In the quiet dawn, hopes arise,
Gentle whispers in soft skies.
Nature's breath, a sweet embrace,
Embracing change, a tender grace.

Petals fall, life starts anew,
Colors burst, a vibrant hue.
Morning light breaks through the haze,
Illuminating fresh pathways.

Echoes of Broken Strings

Silence lingers, hearts collide,
Melodies that once confide.
Distant echoes fade away,
Leaving shadows in their sway.

Ghosts of music haunt the night,
Fingers ache to find the light.
Dreams once woven start to fray,
Yet hope beckons to stay.

Fragments of a New Dawn

Whispers rise with morning sun,
Fractured dreams now come undone.
Splintered pieces, soft and bright,
Craft new visions in the light.

Stars retreat, their work fulfilled,
While restless hearts wait to be thrilled.
Awakening feels strangely near,
Each moment blooming, crystal clear.

Reconstructing the Soul's Mosaic

Shattered tiles in colors bold,
Stories whisper, yet untold.
Fragments dance, a vibrant scheme,
Piecing together a tender dream.

Each setback paints a richer hue,
From chaos, beauty breaks through.
Mosaic crafted with care and tears,
A tapestry woven through all our fears.

Threads of Resilience

In shadows deep, we weave our fate,
With every challenge, we elevate.
Through storms we stand, united and strong,
Our spirits soar, where we belong.

With every tear, a lesson learned,
Through trials faced, our passion burned.
Together bound, we find the light,
In darkest nights, we shine so bright.

Canvas of Colors Unfurled

Brushstrokes dance across the span,
Each hue whispers a gentle plan.
From twilight's glow to morning's dew,
A tapestry of vivid view.

Each color tells a story grand,
Of earth and sky, of sea and sand.
We paint our dreams with vibrant care,
A canvas rich beyond compare.

Rising Tides of Love

In every wave, our hearts collide,
With every ebb, we turn the tide.
The ocean speaks of joy and pain,
Yet through it all, love will remain.

From distant shores, we feel the pull,
A shared heartbeat, forever full.
As tides rise high, we float and soar,
In love's embrace, we crave for more.

Strained Strings

The strings are tight, yet music flows,
From heart to bow, emotion glows.
In every note, a story sings,
Embracing life, through fleeting things.

In moments frail, we find our way,
Through strain and stretch, we learn to play.
The symphony of hopes and fears,
Resonates through laughter and tears.

Beautiful Melodies

In whispered tunes beneath the stars,
We find a joy that heals our scars.
Each melody, a balm for soul,
In harmony, we feel made whole.

With every chord, the heart connects,
In music's weave, love resurrects.
Beautiful echoes fill the air,
A symphony of life to share.

Embracing the Aftermath

In shadows deep, we find our way,
Through echoes of the past, we sway.
With weary hearts, we gather light,
Embracing truths that shine so bright.

The storm has passed, yet whispers stay,
Reminding us of yesterday.
We learn to walk on fractured ground,
Where strength and hope can both be found.

The silence speaks of battles won,
Of mourning lost and rising sun.
We gather pieces, heal the scars,
While gazing fondly at the stars.

New chapters form from ashes gray,
In every end, there lies a play.
We dance within the twilight's glow,
And cherish all we've come to know.

The aftermath, a tender muse,
In every heart, the strength to choose.
With open arms, we greet the morn,
For in our pain, our spirits are born.

Tides of Change

The ocean's pulse, it ebbs and flows,
Transforming shores where the wild wind blows.
Each wave a whisper, a hint of fate,
In endless dance, we contemplate.

Mountains shift while rivers bend,
In nature's grasp, beginnings blend.
What once was firm may fade away,
Yet beauty thrives in fresh array.

The seasons turn, from warm to cold,
As stories of the earth unfold.
In every dawn, a chance to grow,
As winds of change begin to blow.

We stand as trees, both firm and free,
Rooted deep in shared history.
Branches reach for skies above,
In change, we find the strength of love.

Embrace the tides that come and go,
Let rhythms of the world bestow.
For in each shift, new paths emerge,
And hearts awaken, grow, and surge.

The Phoenix's Embrace

From ashes cold, a spark ignites,
A tale of courage, soaring heights.
With wings outstretched, it breaks the night,
The phoenix rises, brave and bright.

In fiery dance, it finds its grace,
Each flicker glows, each ember's trace.
Rebirth in flames, the cycle spins,
In every loss, a chance begins.

Through trials faced, it learns to soar,
With every fall, it seeks for more.
In molten heart, resilience lies,
A testament that never dies.

With every dawn, a new refrain,
From darkened skies, it breaks the chain.
In vibrant hues, it paints the sky,
The phoenix sings, its spirit high.

Embrace the flames that light the way,
For from the dark, we greet the day.
In each rebirth, the promise waits,
To find the strength that love creates.

Moments of Rejuvenation

In quiet hours, we pause to breathe,
Among the whispers, the heart's reprieve.
The sun dips low, the sky ablaze,
In fleeting moments, we find our ways.

Among the trees, the shadows play,
In nature's arms, we drift and sway.
With every leaf that falls and turns,
A spark within our spirit burns.

We taste the rain, its gentle kiss,
In puddles formed, a world of bliss.
With every drop, we shed the weight,
And dance anew, no room for hate.

The dawn awakens, fresh and bright,
A canvas spread for dreams in flight.
In small delights, we craft our days,
And find our joy in myriad ways.

Rejuvenate, let worries fade,
Embrace the light that time has made.
For in the now, our hearts align,
In moments sweet, our souls entwine.

Resilience in the Ashes

In shadows deep, we find our might,
From embers low, we soar to light.
The past ignites, a lesson learned,
In every fall, new fire is burned.

Rise like phoenix, strong and free,
From ruins born, a new decree.
With every tear, a seed we sow,
In ashes warm, our spirits grow.

Through darkest nights, we hold our hopes,
With silent strength, we learn to cope.
Together bound, through thick and thin,
Our hearts ignite, the fight begins.

Though storms may rage and winds may howl,
We stand as one, united, proud.
From fragile roots, we claim the day,
Resilience guides our destined way.

Unraveled Yet Whole

Threads of life woven so fine,
Unraveled dreams in tangled lines.
Yet in the fray, we find our grace,
A tapestry in every place.

Pieces lost, but never gone,
In each heartbreak, new truths dawn.
We stitch the past with love and care,
Embracing all, the joy and despair.

In brokenness, we learn to rise,
To find our strength beneath the skies.
A resilient heart, a boundless soul,
In every fracture, we feel whole.

With open arms, we greet the day,
For every wound, a chance to sway.
With every step, we start anew,
Unraveled yet, our spirits grew.

The Garden of Second Chances

In soil rich, new dreams take root,
A garden blooms, where pasts dispute.
Each seed of hope, a tale untold,
In gentle hands, new futures hold.

Beneath the sun, old shadows fade,
With every rain, the fears invade.
Yet through the struggle, flowers thrive,
In every heart, the will to strive.

The thorns may prick, but still we bloom,
In tangled paths, we find our room.
With every breath, the light we chase,
In this garden, we find our place.

For every fault, a chance to mend,
To plant the seeds that love can send.
In unity, we rise and dance,
In the garden of our second chance.

A Symphony of Rebirth

In silence born, the dawn anew,
A symphony begins to brew.
With whispered notes that fill the air,
A melody beyond compare.

Each note a story, rich and bright,
From shadows deep, we seek the light.
With every chord, our hearts align,
In harmony, our spirits shine.

Through trials faced, the music swells,
In every challenge, courage dwells.
With hands entwined, we sing our song,
Together bound, where we belong.

The rhythm brings us joy and peace,
In every heartbeat, love's increase.
With every breath, a chance to grow,
In this grand symphony, we flow.

Shattered Dreams

In the silence, echoes cry,
Fragments fall from the sky.
Promises that once gleamed bright,
Now lost in endless night.

Hope can wane like fading light,
Leaving shadows in its flight.
Dreams that danced are now on hold,
Whispers of a life untold.

Yet in cracks, new seeds may sprout,
From the dark we'll find a route.
Every shatter tells a tale,
Of resilience that won't fail.

Renewed Visions

Through the haze, a spark ignites,
Guiding eyes to distant heights.
Clouds disperse, revealing skies,
Where the heart learns how to rise.

Once confined in shadows deep,
Now I wake from restless sleep.
Visions bright with colors bold,
Stories waiting to be told.

With each dawn, potential stirs,
Whispers of the life it blurs.
From the ashes, futures glow,
In the light, new dreams will grow.

Mending the Invisible

Hearts wear scars we cannot see,
Silent battles waged to be.
Threads of hope weave through the fray,
Binding wounds in a new way.

Gentle hands, a healing touch,
Remind us that we are enough.
In the quiet, strength will bloom,
As darkness fades, dispelling gloom.

We rise to face a brand new day,
Mending paths that slipped away.
With each stitch, we redefine,
Invisible threads intertwine.

From Ashes to Embrace

Where the fire once burned hot,
Footprints mark the battle fought.
From the ashes, life is born,
Each new dawn, a promise sworn.

Ember dreams whisper and weave,
In the heart, we dare believe.
Beauty grows from charred remains,
Courage born from deepest pains.

In the warmth of the new flame,
Fear dissolves, we're not the same.
From the ruins, strength we find,
In the act of being kind.

Whispers of Reclamation

Through the echoes of the night,
Voices call, a guiding light.
Lost in fear, we find our way,
Yearning for a brighter day.

Reclamation of our song,
Healing where we once felt wrong.
With our choices, we reclaim,
Every heartbeat sings our name.

In the whispers of the breeze,
Restored faith brings us to ease.
Together we can rise and shine,
In unity, our spirits twine.

The Canvas of Tomorrow

Brush strokes of hope and dreams,
Colors bright, bursting at seams.
Each choice a hue, a place to start,
In this vast canvas, we play our part.

Future waits with open arms,
In our hands, we find the charms.
Painting life with every glance,
Every moment, a chance to dance.

Dreams like rivers gracefully flow,
Merging paths where we wish to go.
With each line, we leave a trace,
Creating beauty in this space.

A vision clear, our spirits soar,
Transcending doubts, forevermore.
With every stroke, we'll redefine,
The canvas of tomorrow, yours and mine.

The Art of Picking Up Pieces

Shattered dreams on the cold ground,
Fragments of joy, lost but found.
With gentle hands, we start to mend,
This art of healing, no clear end.

Each broken shard, a story told,
A journey forged in courage bold.
Finding strength in what remains,
Emerging beauty from the pains.

Time, the brush that smooths the edges,
Healing hearts, building new pledges.
From the wreckage, we will rise,
A masterpiece that never dies.

Collaborate with the scars we wear,
Transforming wounds into a prayer.
The art of picking up the pieces,
A collage of hope, love never ceases.

Blossoms Underneath the Ruins

Amidst the rubble, life breaks through,
Tiny blossoms, bright and true.
Nature's will, resilient grace,
Emerging beauty in this place.

Cracked concrete, yet hope resides,
In every petal, the spirit bides.
Colors vivid against the grey,
Whispers of life in disarray.

Each bloom a testament to time,
In adversity, we find our rhyme.
Fragile beauty among the scars,
Shining brightly like the stars.

Buried deep, the past remains,
Yet from the earth, new life gains.
Blossoms flourish, ever brave,
Underneath the ruins, we save.

Secrets of the Rising Sun

Morning light dances on the sea,
Whispers secrets, wild and free.
Golden rays unveil the day,
Promising hope in every way.

With each dawn, the past transforms,
Shadows fade, revealing norms.
Nature's canvas painted bright,
Secrets hidden in its light.

The sun awakens dreams anew,
In its warmth, the world feels true.
Every beam a story's breath,
In its presence, fear meets death.

Listen closely as it rises,
In the silence, wisdom lies.
Secrets of the rising sun,
In its glow, we all are one.

Rebuilding the Bridge

Upon the river's edge we stand,
With broken dreams and fractured land.
We gather stones from yesterday,
To pave a path, to find our way.

Hands reach across the tangled span,
A whisper of hope, a gentle plan.
Together we will weave a thread,
To bridge the gaps where once we fled.

Each plank we lay, a story told,
Of love and loss and hearts of gold.
Through storms that raged, we're weathered still,
With faith and strength, we climb the hill.

The echoes of the past may fade,
But in our hearts, the bond is made.
We'll walk this path with heads held high,
Rebuilding dreams beneath the sky.

Threads of Forgiveness

In silent rooms where shadows dwell,
We weave our tales, a secret spell.
With needle fine and heart sincere,
We stitch together wounds we fear.

Each thread a line, a gentle start,
To mend the bonds that broke apart.
As colors blend in soft embrace,
We find our way to healing space.

Forgiveness whispers, soft and clear,
A tapestry of love draws near.
For in our hearts, the past unwinds,
And grace remakes what time confines.

So take my hand and hold it tight,
We'll weave a future, rich and bright.
With every stitch, a promise new,
Threads of forgiveness, me and you.

Yesterday's Shadows

In twilight's grasp, the shadows play,
Echoes of words that drifted away.
Memories linger, like ghosts in flight,
Dancing on edges of fading light.

The whispers haunt, like fleeting dreams,
Rippling softly in silver streams.
Yet in the dark, a spark ignites,
A longing heart for new heights.

We carry burdens, heavy and old,
Tales of sorrow yet to be told.
But dawn approaches, breaking through,
A canvas waits for vibrant hues.

Leave yesterday beneath the trees,
Where shadows fade with the evening breeze.
Embrace the dawn and let it show,
The path ahead where dreams can grow.

Tomorrow's Light

With every sunrise, hope takes flight,
Casting aside the cloak of night.
The world awakens, fresh and clear,
Inviting dreams to draw us near.

We gather strength from silent hours,
As petals bloom in fragrant showers.
In every heartbeat, futures blend,
A dance of magic we extend.

With eyes wide open, we will see,
The endless possibilities.
For every moment holds a key,
Unlock the doors to what can be.

So take a step into the dawn,
Leave doubts and fears forever gone.
For in tomorrow's warm embrace,
We find our truth, our rightful place.

Radiance Amidst the Rubble

From ashes rise a fervent flame,
In broken places, hope will claim.
Through crumbled walls and shattered ground,
A vibrant pulse is often found.

The wreckage tells our story true,
Of battles fought and lessons due.
Yet in the chaos, light will gleam,
A testament to every dream.

Each shard reflects a change in state,
Where endings bloom and hearts elate.
Connected still, though torn apart,
We build anew, ignite the heart.

Let not despair define this space,
For beauty thrives in time and grace.
With every step, we rise once more,
Radiance shines, forevermore.

The Architecture of Healing

In whispers soft, the heart begins,
To mend the cracks, to heal the sins.
With every breath, a new design,
A fortress built where love can shine.

Brick by brick, the soul restores,
Each memory laid, new open doors.
Bridges crossed with gentle care,
A path of strength, a life laid bare.

Among the scars that tell the tale,
Hope rises high, it will not fail.
The walls may breathe with silent sighs,
But in this space, the spirit flies.

Through echoes of the past we tread,
We carve a future, gently led.
Each wound a lesson, deeply sown,
In the architecture, we have grown.

Beyond the Shattered Mirror

Fragments glisten in the light,
Reflections dance, but not in fright.
Each shard a story, a lesson learned,
In silent strength, the heart discerned.

Beyond the surface, meaning hides,
In brokenness, the truth abides.
We piece together dreams once lost,
Embracing shadows, no matter the cost.

The mirror's edge may cut so deep,
But in the pain, we start to leap.
A new facade, a wiser gaze,
Transforms the dark into a blaze.

Discovering beauty carved by fate,
In scattered moments, we create.
A vision clear, though cracks remain,
Beyond the mirror, love will reign.

Navigating Through Silent Storms

The winds may howl, the skies may weep,
In silent storms, our burdens steep.
But through the chaos, strength is found,
In currents fierce, we stand our ground.

With eyes wide open, hearts aligned,
We sail through tempests, intertwined.
Each wave a lesson, tide a guide,
In depths of sorrow, we will rise.

The silence screams in thunder's hush,
Yet in the quiet, we feel the rush.
A clearer path begins to show,
Through the uncertain, we bravely row.

Though shadows loom with stormy breath,
We craft our journey, defying death.
And when the sun breaks through the gloom,
We'll dance upon the waves of bloom.

Tides of Transformation

The oceans shift with every dream,
In the ebb and flow, we find our theme.
With each new wave, we dive anew,
Into the depths of what is true.

Transformation calls in whispered waves,
As shells of old, the spirit saves.
Through changing tides, the heart gives way,
To horizons fresh, the dawn of day.

Beneath the surface, treasures lie,
In depths unseen, we learn to fly.
The tides may rise with trials steep,
Yet in their rhythm, dreams we keep.

With open arms, we greet the flow,
Embracing change, we come to know.
The dance of life, a sacred rite,
In tides of transformation, we find light.

From Ruins to Radiance

Amid the rubble, whispers rise,
Hope reborn beneath gray skies.
With every crack, a seed of light,
From ruins grows a future bright.

Shadows fade, the dawn draws near,
New beginnings, pause and hear.
The stones that once bore heavy pain,
Now cradle dreams where love will reign.

Through ashes, life will start anew,
A vibrant canvas, painted true.
Each scar tells tales of battle won,
From ruins, radiant hearts become.

Beneath the weight of yesterday,
Emerges strength with each display.
A phoenix soaring, fierce and bold,
From ruins, stories yet untold.

In every heart, a spark remains,
Transforming loss to rich refrains.
From ashes, vibrant colors bloom,
From ruins rises, light consumes.

Whispers of Renewal

In softest breeze, hear secrets shared,
The earth awakens, gently bared.
Each note of spring a tender song,
In whispers of renewal, we belong.

The rustling leaves, a soft embrace,
Nature's breath, a sacred space.
From silent ground, life starts to creep,
In whispers of renewal, dreams take leap.

A budding flower, crisp and bright,
Emerges from the cloak of night.
Each petal glistens, freshly born,
In whispers of renewal, hope is sworn.

The rivers flow with stories deep,
Of ancient hills where silence weeps.
Yet from the depths, the voices soar,
In whispers of renewal, life restores.

With every pulse, the world awakes,
In harmony, the earth partakes.
As dawn unfolds with colors wide,
In whispers of renewal, we abide.

A Journey Beyond the Fracture

Across the chasm, shadows fall,
A journey beckons, heed the call.
With fractured paths, yet hearts aligned,
Beyond the break, new ways we find.

Each step forward, courage grows,
In brokenness, the beauty shows.
With every stumble, lessons learned,
A journey taken, passion burned.

Through twisted trails, the light will guide,
With strength in numbers, side by side.
Emerging from the shard-strewn pain,
A journey bold, no loss in vain.

From fragments, tapestry we weave,
In unity, we dare believe.
With open hearts, we seek the sun,
A journey shared, each soul as one.

Beyond the fracture, freedom sings,
Resilience finds its truest wings.
Together, onward we shall soar,
A journey rich in dreams and more.

The Colors of Second Chances

In twilight shades of dusk's embrace,
Colors blend in sacred space.
Mistakes once made, now brushes bold,
The colors dance, their stories told.

Each stroke a tale of lessons learned,
In brighter hues, the passion burned.
A palette rich with every hue,
The colors shine, a life anew.

In every fall, a chance to rise,
With open hearts beneath vast skies.
Embrace the flaws and weave them tight,
The colors spark in darkest night.

From gray to gold, the shades will shift,
In every heart, the power to uplift.
Second chances, vibrant and true,
The colors bloom, refreshed in view.

With every dawn, rebirth begins,
Through every loss, a strength within.
The colors of hope painted wide,
In second chances, love will abide.

The Bridge from Brokenness

In shadows deep, we find our way,
Step by step, through night and day.
Each crack a story, each scar a sign,
Of bridges built through love's design.

With trembling hands, we reach for light,
The warmth of hope, a dawn so bright.
In every tear, a lesson learned,
In every heart, a fire burned.

We gather stones, the past we mend,
From shattered dreams, new paths we send.
In every struggle, we rise anew,
A bridge from brokenness, strong and true.

Together we cross on faith's own beam,
Toward a future, a vibrant dream.
No longer lost in the dark abyss,
We'll walk with courage, in joy, in bliss.

So take a breath, let go of fear,
On this bridge, our hearts draw near.
For in our healing, we find our place,
A journey shared, a sweet embrace.

Harvesting Hope from Tears

From sorrow's soil, we plant the seeds,
In every tear, a new heart bleeds.
We gather strength, begin to grow,
In fields of hope, where love can flow.

The storm may rage, the dark may fall,
Yet through the pain, we hear the call.
With every drop, a lesson sown,
In the garden of the heart, we're shown.

Sunshine breaks, the clouds disperse,
In this life, we rewrite the verse.
With gentle love, we tend the ground,
In silent whispers, new joys found.

We take our time, with tender care,
And nurture dreams, both rich and rare.
From weary nights and endless days,
We harvest hope in countless ways.

So when the night tries to confine,
Remember the seeds that intertwine.
In the chamber of the heart, let tears flow,
For they will guide us where hope can grow.

Tangled Roots

In the earth, our roots entwine,
Beneath the surface, stories line.
Through trials faced, we learn to stand,
In tangled webs, a steady hand.

Though storms may shake, and shadows loom,
Our roots reach deep, dispelling gloom.
Together in strength, we weather strife,
In every struggle, we find our life.

Nourished by love, we stretch and grow,
In life's vast garden, together we sow.
Through thick and thin, we intertwine,
Tangled roots, a bond divine.

With every twitch, a silent prayer,
In unity, we breathe the air.
For even in chaos, we stand tall,
With tangled roots, we will not fall.

So let us thrive, through every change,
In life's embrace, sweet and strange.
Together we flourish, a dance, a tune,
With tangled roots, we'll reach for the moon.

Flourishing Leaves

In the embrace of gentle winds,
Where laughter sways, and the heart begins,
Flourishing leaves in vibrant hues,
Dance in the light, they share their views.

From whispered secrets of the earth,
Each leaf a story, each breeze a birth.
In the warmth of sun, they stretch and sway,
Painting the sky in a bright array.

With every rustle, they sing a song,
Of resilience found where they belong.
For in the stillness, their spirits rise,
Flourishing leaves beneath vast skies.

When storms may come, and shadows creep,
The sturdy branches begin to weep.
Yet even then, they'll hold their ground,
In blooming beauty, strength is found.

So let us learn from leafy grace,
To find our joy in every place.
For like the leaves, we too can thrive,
In the light of love, together alive.

Echoing Through Time

Whispers of the past draw near,
In shadows long, they reappear.
Faded echoes in the night,
Guiding souls with gentle light.

Time's tapestry unwinds,
Memories in rhythm, intertwined.
Footsteps soft on ancient stone,
In the heart, they find a home.

History's breath upon the breeze,
Stories told among the trees.
Fragments of a life once lived,
In every heart, a story gives.

Moments linger, forever tied,
In whispers where the secrets hide.
Each heartbeat synchronized,
With the past where love resides.

Through the ages, voices soar,
Carrying tales forevermore.
In the silence, truths unfold,
Echoes of the brave and bold.

The Canvas of Repair

Brushstrokes on a canvas bare,
Colors blend with tender care.
What was broken now can mend,
Artisan hands that gently tend.

Fragments scattered on the floor,
Hope emerges, seeking more.
Each piece fitting into place,
Rebuilding dreams with patient grace.

In shadows lies a bright design,
Crafting paths where hearts align.
Repairing not just what is seen,
But the spirit's core, serene.

Stitches formed in golden threads,
Linking stories that love spreads.
Every mark a tale to tell,
Of how we rise, how we fell.

A masterpiece of life anew,
With every hue, we find what's true.
The canvas, worn, now full of light,
A symbol of our endless fight.

A Symphony of Second Chances

In every note, a chance reborn,
A melody so sweet, not worn.
With echoes of a missed refrain,
Resilient hearts embrace the pain.

Harmonies that rise and fall,
Soft reminders of our call.
In tuning, we find our way,
To brighter dreams and a new day.

The rhythm of the hopeful beat,
Embracing sorrow, bittersweet.
With each return, a lesson learned,
In the flames, our spirits burned.

A symphony of voices blend,
In unity, our hearts ascend.
Together we create, we dare,
To seize the moments, bold and rare.

Through trials faced, we take our stand,
With open hearts and outstretched hands.
The music plays, we rise anew,
In every note, a chance for you.

Transcending the Tides

Waves crash down with forceful might,
Yet within lies a soft light.
The ocean's song, a potent grace,
Carries dreams to distant space.

As currents shift and patterns change,
We learn to bend, to rearrange.
With every ebb and flow, we grow,
Finding where our spirits go.

In the depths, the secrets lie,
Beneath the vast and endless sky.
Transcending fears, embracing dreams,
In harmony with nature's schemes.

Drifting on a sea of stars,
We heal the wounds, erase the scars.
In every rise and fall of tide,
We uncover strength inside.

Through the surges, we will glide,
In unity, our hopes collide.
For in the dance of sea and wind,
A journey starts, and love will mend.

Reclaiming the Unbroken Spirit

In whispers soft, the heart takes flight,
Reviving dreams beneath the night.
A spark ignites, a fire burns,
With every step, the spirit yearns.

Through scars we wear, the stories flow,
In every tear, the strength to grow.
Unbroken chains, we rise and stand,
United now, in freedom's hand.

Each shadow cast, a lesson learned,
In quiet moments, courage turned.
Voices echo, calling clear,
A symphony of hope draws near.

With every challenge, grace we find,
In fractured places, hearts aligned.
We weave anew, the threads of fate,
With open hearts, we elevate.

Reclaim the night, embrace the light,
A journey born of endless fight.
With every breath, we hold our claim,
In unity, we rise in flame.

New Patterns on Worn Canvas

In gentle strokes, colors blend,
A canvas speaks, where dreams extend.
From faded hues, fresh shades emerge,
With every line, our hearts converge.

Patterns shift, old tales renew,
In whispers deep, the soul breaks through.
Each blemish born, a tale to tell,
In every mark, we learn to dwell.

Brushes dance, in rhythmic flow,
Creating beauty, letting go.
From chaos born, a vision bright,
We find our way, through darkest night.

Textures rise, with life imbued,
In every shade, a spirit renewed.
The canvas waits, our hands invite,
To craft a world, with pure delight.

New patterns form, as we create,
In every heart, a love innate.
Together here, we paint our song,
On worn canvas, where we belong.

Love Beyond the Shadows

In twilight's glow, two hearts align,
A whispered hope, a secret sign.
Beyond the shadows, light takes flight,
In tender grace, we find our might.

Through darkest nights, love brightly gleams,
A beacon warm, in silken dreams.
With every touch, we break the chains,
In silent vows, true love remains.

As dawn unfolds, our fears dissolve,
In unity, we rise and solve.
For love transcends, all shadows cast,
In every moment, a die is cast.

With open souls, we brave the storm,
In fierce embrace, we find our form.
Through trials faced, our hearts stay true,
In love's embrace, we start anew.

Beyond the shadows, we take flight,
Together strong, a radiant light.
In every heartbeat, we proclaim,
A love eternal, wild and untamed.

Reimagining Fractured Futures

In shattered dreams, new visions rise,
A tapestry of hopeful skies.
With every fracture, seeds we sow,
In unity, our spirits grow.

Through broken paths, we carve our way,
In courage found, we seize the day.
With open hearts, we dare to dream,
In fractured futures, hope will gleam.

Each setback met as textbook draws,
In wisdom gained, we find the cause.
With every breath, we stand as one,
In reimagining, our battles won.

From ashes rise, a brighter dawn,
In every heartbeat, we are drawn.
To futures bright, where love commands,
Together weaving, hand in hand.

In fractured dreams, we build anew,
With faith reborn, our vision true.
Reimagined paths, we dare to tread,
Towards a future, brightly spread.

Beyond the Scar

In shadows where fear used to dwell,
A whisper of hope begins to swell.
Each wound, a story etched in time,
Emerging from silence, a strength sublime.

With every heartbeat, resilience grows,
A garden where love's essence flows.
Beyond the pain, the light breaks in,
A journey reborn, the soul's new skin.

Memories linger, yet fade away,
Revealing the dawn of a brighter day.
Through trials faced, we find our way,
Beyond the scar, in freedom we sway.

We gather the pieces, a puzzle complete,
Each fragment unique, our story replete.
In unity's embrace, we rise from despair,
Beyond the scar, we breathe the air.

The echoes of struggle, they teach and release,
A testament forged, from chaos to peace.
Beyond the scar, the future's our art,
Together we flourish, together, we start.

Reimagining Togetherness

In the tapestry woven of dreams and delight,
We gather in circles, hearts shining bright.
Each voice a color, we blend and we share,
Reimagining togetherness, a bond so rare.

With moments of laughter, we paint the day,
In simple connections, we find our way.
Hand in hand, we traverse the path,
Creating a haven that sparks joy and laughs.

When shadows loom and the world feels cold,
Together we gather, our strength to uphold.
In silence we stand, in spirit we soar,
Reimagining togetherness, forevermore.

Through seasons of change, we find our ground,
In shared aspirations, our purpose unbound.
With love as our anchor, we journey ahead,
In the dance of togetherness, our fears we shed.

Each story a thread, we weave with grace,
A united vision in this sacred space.
In the tapestry of life, we craft and we build,
Reimagining togetherness, our spirits fulfilled.

A Tapestry of Tomorrow

In threads of vision, we sow our dreams,
A tapestry woven of hopes and schemes.
Each stitch a promise, a vision to see,
A tapestry of tomorrow, vibrant and free.

Through challenges faced, we learn and we grow,
In the fabric of time, our stories flow.
With hearts intertwined, we build and we mend,
A future unfolding, a journey, a friend.

In colors of courage, we paint the sky,
With whispers of purpose, we reach for the high.
A tapestry bright, with laughter and tears,
Reflecting our triumphs, embracing our fears.

Together we thread, in rhythm and rhyme,
Creating a legacy that echoes through time.
With love as our needle, we stitch every seam,
For tomorrow awaits, with promises gleam.

A canvas of moments, woven with care,
A tapestry of tomorrow, eternally fair.
In unity strong, we boldly embrace,
The future ahead, a beautiful space.

The Dance of Renewal

In circles of grace, we move and we sway,
The dance of renewal ignites the day.
With rhythms of life, we learn to let go,
Embracing the changes that help us to grow.

The past fades away, like shadows at dawn,
In the light of the present, we carry on.
Each step a revival, each heartbeat a chance,
In the dance of renewal, we find our romance.

With every twirl, we shed what we know,
Creating a pathway where new blossoms grow.
The music of hope resounds in the air,
Inviting our spirits to dance without care.

Together we rise, like waves on the sea,
In harmony's embrace, we are truly free.
The dance of renewal, a circle complete,
With love as our guide, we sway to the beat.

In the rhythm of life, we find our way home,
Through trials and triumphs, we never roam alone.
The dance of renewal, forever it flows,
Uniting our hearts, where true beauty grows.

Rewoven Narratives

Threads of stories entwine anew,
In every heartbeat, truth shines through.
Whispers of past and future collide,
Together we walk, side by side.

Echoes of laughter, shadows of pain,
Woven in fabric, joy and disdain.
Every chapter crafted with care,
A tapestry rich beyond compare.

In moments of silence, voices emerge,
From the depths of sorrow, new tales surge.
Each flicker of light, a beacon so bright,
Guiding us forward, through the night.

Let us celebrate every unique thread,
For in our stories, we are led.
The beauty lies in the tales we weave,
Interwoven destinies, we believe.

Together we compose, a song so profound,
In the silence between, our hearts resound.
Rewoven narratives, a bond so rare,
In unity's arms, we find our prayer.

Journeys Through Unseen Valleys

In the shadows where dreams take flight,
We wander softly, guided by light.
Footsteps echo on paths yet unsown,
With courage and hope, we brave the unknown.

Valleys unseen, where whispers reside,
Life's gentle lessons in silence confide.
Every detour unveils a new view,
And hearts awaken to wonders anew.

Underneath stars, we find our way home,
Through valleys and hills, we choose to roam.
Hands joined together, we step side by side,
In the journeys that shape us, we confide.

With every heartbeat, a story unfolds,
In journeys through valleys, our spirit upholds.
Embrace the unknown, let courage renew,
For every adventure leads us to you.

Through unseen paths, our souls intertwine,
A dance of connection, a love so divine.
The journey is rich, its tapestry spun,
In the unseen valleys, we find the one.

Kindling the Flame of Connection

A flicker ignites, deep within the night,
It calls out to hearts, a beacon of light.
In whispers and glances, connections are found,
As kindred spirits weave bonds profound.

Through laughter and tears, we share our truth,
Moments of joy, the essence of youth.
With every heartbeat, the flame grows bright,
Kindling the warmth, chasing away fright.

In the tapestry woven of trust and grace,
We find our belonging, a sacred space.
Each story shared, a spark to ignite,
In the flames of connection, we take flight.

Dancing together through shadows and light,
Our spirits entwined, in the still of the night.
For every heart reached is a gift we bestow,
Kindling the flame, making love grow.

In every embrace, we gather our dreams,
Through kindling the flame, the universe beams.
Together we'll nurture this fire so bright,
For connection unites us, a beautiful sight.

Saluting the Spirit of Renewal

As dawn breaks anew, a promise is made,
In the heart of the earth, old layers fade.
With each rising sun, a canvas unfolds,
Saluting the spirit that courage upholds.

In whispers of wind, the past gently sighs,
In the glow of the morn, the future replies.
Breaking old chains, we rise from the ground,
With seeds of renewal, life's beauty is found.

Together we dance, beneath skies of blue,
Rebirth in our veins, we bind ourselves too.
Each step forward, a tribute to grace,
Honoring journeys, each unique pace.

Embrace the new growth, let go of the old,
For renewal's embrace is a treasure to hold.
In every heartbeat, the spirit will rise,
Saluting the dawn and the limitless skies.

In harmony singing, we rise and we soar,
With hope in our hearts, we open the door.
To futures unwritten, our spirits entwined,
Saluting renewal, a love redefined.

Springing from the Ground Up

Beneath the soil, life waits, unseen,
Roots intertwine in the dark, so keen.
Sprouts push through, breaking the crust,
Emerging bright, in sun they trust.

Whispers of green fill the air,
Dancing petals, without a care.
Life's cycle spins, a vibrant art,
From humble seeds, hopes restart.

Each drop of rain, a soft embrace,
Nature's work, a sacred space.
Tiny wonders grow bold and loud,
Springing forth, a joyful crowd.

Colors burst in festival bright,
Morning dew, diamonds in light.
With the warmth, we start to thrive,
In the garden, we come alive.

So let us cherish, tend, and nurture,
Tune to the rhythm of nature's allure.
Springing from the ground in delight,
Life awakens, day turns to night.

From Silence to Song

In shadows deep, where whispers lay,
A gentle hush begins to sway.
From muted thoughts, a spark ignites,
Rising softly, it takes flight.

Notes of dawn, sweet melodies fold,
Tales of beauty silently told.
Echoing through the morning air,
A symphony found, beyond compare.

Hushed hearts listen, tuning in close,
Voices awaken, each note, a dose.
From silence, a chorus begins to bloom,
Chasing away the lingering gloom.

Strings of longing, soft as a sigh,
Winds carry tunes that soar and fly.
Harmony breaks through the night,
Turning quiet into pure light.

So give ear to what life can sing,
In every moment, joy can spring.
From silence to song, we find our place,
A melody woven in time's embrace.

Shaping Tomorrow's Echoes

In every choice, a ripple flows,
Seeds of tomorrow, gently sows.
Paths untaken, we carve anew,
Each step forward, a world in view.

Voices raised in unity loud,
Dreams ignited, beneath the shroud.
Together we shape the years to come,
With every beat, hear the drum.

Courage takes root, breaks through the stone,
In solidarity, we are never alone.
Building bridges where shadows fall,
Hope intertwined, answering the call.

Moments stitched with threads of light,
In every heart, a future bright.
What we nurture today, we reap,
Shaping echoes, our promise to keep.

So lift your gaze, see what's ahead,
With open hearts and dreams widespread.
Shaping tomorrow with every thought,
In the tapestry of life, we're caught.

The Light Within the Fracture

Amidst the cracks, a shimmer glows,
A testament to what life knows.
In brokenness, we find our might,
From fractured paths, emerges light.

Shattered pieces form a new design,
With every wound, a chance to shine.
Resilience blooms in darkest hour,
Finding strength within our power.

Fragments tell a story, raw and clear,
Echoes of laughter, whispers of fear.
What once was lost, now we reclaim,
In every fracture, we find our name.

Illuminated scars tell of grace,
Carved in time, a sacred space.
From every struggle, wisdom grows,
In shadows cast, the brightness shows.

So embrace the light where it breaks through,
In every split, the true and the new.
The light within, a guiding star,
Transforming us, no matter how far.

Foundations of a Flickering Flame

In the quiet dusk, a spark ignites,
A gentle whisper of shared delights.
With kindred hearts, we gather near,
Building dreams, erasing fear.

Through the shadows, our laughter flows,
Breaking barriers, love grows.
Together we stand, warm and bright,
Foundations strong, glowing light.

The winds may howl, but we hold tight,
In the storm, we find our might.
Each flicker tells a tale profound,
In unity, our solace found.

Time may test the ties we've worn,
Yet in the fire, we are reborn.
With every ember, hope remains,
In the heart's hearth, love sustains.

So let us nurture this blazing cheer,
For in our bond, we persevere.
With every flame, our story glows,
In warmth and trust, forever flows.

Embers of New Beginnings

In the ashes of yesterday's dreams,
New life stirs, or so it seems.
With courage, we rise from the ground,
In the twilight, hope is found.

Each breath we take, a chance to grow,
Seeds of potential start to sow.
With open hearts, we face tomorrow,
Turning scars into bright arrows.

Embers dance in twilight's embrace,
Whispers of fate in a sacred space.
From the struggles, a path we weave,
In the moment, we choose to believe.

The light within guides every choice,
In the silence, we hear our voice.
With every step, a story unfolds,
In the warmth of dreams, we are consoled.

Let us cherish this journey's worth,
In the tapestry of rebirth.
With hope as our North Star, we trace,
The beautiful lines of our embrace.

Wandering Souls, Finding Home

In the vastness, we roam so free,
Searching for where we're meant to be.
With weary hearts and tired feet,
In the distance, our dreams meet.

Every journey leads to a sigh,
Under the canvas of endless sky.
With each step on this winding road,
The truth of belonging is slowly bestowed.

Through the chaos, a calm unfolds,
In the stories of the brave and bold.
Wandering souls, we seek the light,
In the shadows, we find our fight.

Beyond the hills and rivers wide,
Home is where our hearts abide.
In laughter shared and love returned,
The lessons of life are brightly learned.

As the dawn breaks, clarity flows,
In the embrace of loved ones, we close.
Wandering no more, we finally see,
In each other, we've found the key.

Reweaving the Fabric of Affection

Threads of love in a tapestry weave,
Moments cherished, we dare to believe.
With every knot, the bond grows strong,
In patterns of warmth, we all belong.

Through trials faced, our colors blend,
In the fabric of life, together we mend.
Each stitch a memory, rich and bright,
In the heart's loom, we craft our light.

As seasons shift, the design will change,
Yet the spirit remains, never estranged.
In loops of laughter, in tears we share,
We reweave love with tender care.

Though frayed at times, we unite the seams,
In the quiet moments, we fulfill dreams.
With every thread, a promise made,
In this embrace, we are remade.

So let us cherish this quilt of grace,
In the warmth of hearts, we find our place.
Together we weave, together we grow,
In the fabric of affection, forever we'll glow.

Fragments of Renewal

In whispers soft, the dawn awakes,
With golden hues the skyline breaks.
Fragments of dreams in morning light,
A canvas fresh, reborn from night.

Each petal shakes off winter's chill,
The earth exhales, revived at will.
Life stirs anew in gentle grace,
Nature's rhythm, a warm embrace.

With every breath, the heart expands,
In quiet strength, the spirit stands.
From ashes cold, the fire glows,
A promise found where hope still grows.

The river flows, its course defined,
Through valleys deep, with joy entwined.
In every drop, a story told,
Of time unbroken, brave and bold.

As shadows fade, the light will guide,
Through restless seas, the waves collide.
Yet in the storm, a spark remains,
A symphony of life's refrains.

Resilience in Tenderness

In tender hearts, a strength ignites,
A fragile force that softly fights.
Like whispers shared in quiet night,
Resilience blooms, a guiding light.

With gentle hands, the world we mold,
In every story, love is bold.
Through trials faced and tears we shed,
We stand as one, while others fled.

The roots run deep, though winds may rage,
In unity, we turn the page.
From brokenness, we learn to rise,
To find our strength in soft goodbyes.

With every fall, we find our ground,
In whispered hopes, the lost are found.
Each heartbeat sings of what's to come,
A melody that makes us one.

Through gentle storms and fragile air,
We carry dreams beyond despair.
In tenderness, we find our fire,
A spark ignited, rising higher.

Echoes of Restoration

Among the trees, the silence hums,
Echoes of life where stillness comes.
Restoration whispers through the leaves,
In every branch, the past believes.

The river's flow, a soft embrace,
Reflects the scars upon the face.
Yet from the depths of every storm,
A tranquil heart begins to warm.

With colors bright, the sunset sighs,
A tapestry in painted skies.
Each hue a promise, bold and clear,
Restoration blooms, a tale sincere.

In every shadow, hope persists,
Through tangled paths, we can't resist.
The echoes call, a sweet refrain,
Reminding us we rise again.

The stars emerge in velvet night,
Guiding lost souls with their light.
In every whisper, every sound,
Restoration lost will soon be found.

The Anatomy of Hope

In every breath, a pulse of light,
The anatomy of hope takes flight.
With every heartbeat, dreams align,
Filling the soul like cherished wine.

In eyes that glimmer, stories shine,
Each moment woven, yours and mine.
The fragile dance of what could be,
Hope blooms like petals on a tree.

With open hands, the future calls,
Through every rise, through every fall.
The tapestry of life unfolds,
In vibrant threads, our strength beholds.

Through darkness deep and endless night,
Emerges dawn, a flash of light.
The anatomy of joy preserves,
In gentle hearts, the world observes.

Each step is bold, though fear may creep,
In hope, we find the will to leap.
With faith as our unwavering guide,
The anatomy of hope will bide.

Heartstrings in Reconstruction

In twilight's glow, we mend the seams,
Each broken thread holds whispered dreams.
With gentle hands, we stitch anew,
A tapestry of love in every hue.

Through storms we've walked, and pain we've known,
Yet in despair, new seeds are sown.
We'll build a bridge from hurt to grace,
And find our strength in warm embrace.

The echoes of the past will fade,
As harmony in heart is made.
Through trials faced, we learn and grow,
In love's embrace, our spirits glow.

Each note we play, a soft refrain,
Turning wounds to wisdom gained.
With every chord, we're intertwined,
Our heartstrings joined, forever aligned.

Reconstruction of the heart's design,
From shattered dreams to paths divine.
Together we rise, hand in hand,
In the symphony we've planned.

Creating Gold from Ashes

In the aftermath of fire's plight,
Hope flickers softly, dim yet bright.
From ashes cold, we gather chance,
To weave our future in fate's dance.

Lessons learned from embers glow,
In every tear, a chance to grow.
We rise from rubble, fierce and bold,
Creating gold from stories told.

The past may haunt, but we stand strong,
With hearts ablaze, we sing our song.
Out of despair, beauty will bloom,
Resilience finds its place, no room.

In shadows cast, our spirits spark,
Reflecting light amidst the dark.
With every step, we chase the sun,
Together forged, we've just begun.

From ashes high, we reach the skies,
With open hearts, we dare to rise.
Through trials faced, our dreams expand,
In unity, we take a stand.

Resilience's Thundering Echo

In valleys deep where silence dwells,
The echoes rise, the courage swells.
Resilience roars, a fierce embrace,
Through storms encountered, we find grace.

Each challenge met, with strength we wear,
In every heartbeat, hope laid bare.
With thunder's voice, we claim our ground,
In the tapestry of life, we're found.

Through shadows cast, we journey on,
With spirits high, our fears are gone.
In shared breaths, we craft our might,
Resilience shines, a guiding light.

For every fall, we rise once more,
With passion fierce, we dare to soar.
The thundering echoes, loud and clear,
Resilience sings, we hold it dear.

In unity, we find our way,
Through trials faced, come what may.
With love's embrace, we face the fight,
Together forging strength and light.

Beyond Fragments, We Rise

In shattered pieces, stories dwell,
Each fragment holds a whispered spell.
Beyond the scars, our spirits soar,
For in the cracks, there's so much more.

We gather light from every wound,
In every heart, resilience bloomed.
With open arms, we face the skies,
In unity, beyond fragments, we rise.

Through tempest winds, we find our voice,
In every struggle, we make our choice.
To stand together, hand in hand,
Our hearts aflame, we understand.

Through layers thick, we pave the way,
With every dawn, a bright display.
In echoes deep, we hear the song,
Beyond the pain, we all belong.

From dust to stars, we journey far,
Collecting hope like shining stars.
Embracing all that life bestows,
With love's embrace, our spirit grows.

A Journey Through Ruins

Through shattered halls and faded light,
Echoes of the past take flight.
Whispers linger in the air,
Carrying tales of lost despair.

Worn stones tell their silent lore,
Each crack a path to days of yore.
Nature reclaims what once was grand,
A fragile grip on time's command.

Step by step on ancient floor,
Feel the pulse of memories' core.
Ghostly shadows dance and sway,
Guiding souls who lost their way.

In the silence, hearts connect,
Finding beauty in neglect.
Where beauty blooms from broken dreams,
A journey crafted, or so it seems.

From ruins, hope begins to rise,
Like phoenix soaring through the skies.
Rebirth waits in every stone,
In shadows, we are never alone.

The Power of Repair

In every tear, there's a story spun,
Threads of pain, thread by thread, undone.
With gentle hands, we weave once more,
Finding strength in what we restore.

Cracks in porcelain, gold adorned,
Beauty born from what was scorned.
Life's fragments come, a patchwork fair,
Transforming scars into love's repair.

Each stitch whispers, 'You are whole,'
Mending hearts, reclaiming soul.
A tapestry of all we've known,
In every fracture, seeds are sown.

We gather pieces, once apart,
With patient hands, we mend each heart.
Together we shall find our way,
In every break, a bright new day.

Forging futures through tender art,
In brokenness, we find our start.
The power of repair, a healing song,
Unites the lost, the weak, the strong.

Serendipity in Shambles

Amidst the chaos, chance does gleam,
In tangled pathways, wild dreams teem.
Fortuitous meets with the bizarre,
In shambles, we find who we are.

Twisted paths that fate has drawn,
Unexpected turns at each new dawn.
In the mess, a spark ignites,
Leading hearts to joyful heights.

Laughter echoes through broken trails,
Finding solace where hope prevails.
Serendipity, a gentle guide,
Finding treasure where tear drops hide.

With every stumble, grace will rise,
In tangled webs, we seek the wise.
Through fallen dreams, new visions sprout,
In shattered pieces, there's no doubt.

From shards and fragments, magic brews,
A canvas painted with vibrant hues.
In chaos, we learn to dance and sway,
Serendipity lights the fray.

Crafting Love Anew

From ashes cold, a fire ignites,
Crafting love through gentle nights.
With every word, a bond we weave,
In tender moments, we believe.

Two hearts join in a dance so sweet,
Each step forward, a rhythm discreet.
In laughter shared, and tears we pour,
Love blooms anew, forever more.

Through seasons' change, we find our way,
In every challenge, love will stay.
A journey taken, hand in hand,
Together faced, together we stand.

Painted skies of softest hue,
Crafting dreams, our visions true.
With every kiss, the world expands,
In love's embrace, we make our plans.

With open hearts, we'll face the day,
In every moment, come what may.
Crafting love, a work of art,
A masterpiece within the heart.

Unraveling the Past

In shadows deep, the whispers call,
Memories linger, yet often fall.
Frayed edges of time, a tapestry spun,
Revealing the truths we wish were undone.

With every thread, a story unfolds,
Of laughter, of heartache, of secrets untold.
We sift through the ashes, the remnants remain,
Seeking the wisdom buried in pain.

Ghosts of the choices we've left behind,
Echo in silence, a haunting kind.
Yet through the mists, a light gleams bright,
A guide to the future, a beacon of light.

In the depths of the heart, we search for truth,
Rekindling the flame of our fading youth.
For every regret, a lesson to learn,
A chance to forgive, a bridge to return.

The past is a canvas, colors blend,
Painting a picture, where heartaches mend.
So we'll gather the pieces, stitch them anew,
In the tapestry of life, we'll find our view.

Wings of Resurgence

From ashes we rise, like phoenix in flight,
With courage ignited, we claim the night.
The winds of change whisper soft and low,
Guiding our spirits where we dare to go.

Each scar tells a tale, of battles we've fought,
Of dreams that were shattered, and lessons taught.
Yet hope is a flame that dances and glows,
In the heart of the weary, resilience grows.

We spread our wings wide, embracing the sky,
With every heartbeat, we learn to fly.
Through storms and doubts, we navigate with grace,
Finding our rhythm, reclaiming our space.

The clouds may gather, but we shall not yield,
For strength is our armor, our hearts are our shield.
In the symphony of life, we sing our song,
Together in harmony, where we belong.

Let laughter and love be our guiding quest,
With kindness and courage, we are truly blessed.
A journey of wings, unbound and free,
Together we'll soar, a tapestry.

Reforging the Bonds

In the wake of silence, we find our way,
With whispered intentions, we choose to stay.
A tapestry woven of laughter and tears,
Rekindling connections lost through the years.

Each moment a thread, each smile a stitch,
Embracing the warmth, we weather each glitch.
No distance too great, no wound too deep,
Together we gather the dreams we keep.

Through trials and triumphs, our spirits entwine,
A bond forged in fire, resilient and fine.
With open hearts, we cultivate trust,
In the garden of friendship, love is a must.

In laughter and sorrow, we share our space,
Holding each other in a warm embrace.
With every heartbeat, our hands intertwine,
In the dance of forever, our souls combine.

The echoes of time, they carry us forth,
In the compass of life, we find our worth.
Together we journey, as one we stand tall,
Reforging the bonds that will never fall.

Breathing New Life

Awakening dreams from slumbering night,
With every sunrise, hope takes flight.
The pulse of the earth sings a tune so sweet,
Inviting us gently to rise to our feet.

In gardens of promise, new blossoms arise,
Colors igniting, like vibrant skies.
With each gentle rain, the roots go down,
Grounding our spirits, reclaiming our crown.

The whispers of change dance in the breeze,
Carrying stories of hearts at ease.
We breathe in deeply, the air filled with grace,
Finding our rhythm in this sacred space.

Through trials and tribulations, we learn to transcend,
Embracing the journey, not just the end.
With open horizons, our spirits unite,
Breathing new life into the endless night.

So let us awaken to what lies ahead,
With hearts full of courage, where dreams are fed.
In the tapestry woven with threads of our days,
We breathe new life in so many ways.

Unveiling Strength from Strain

In shadows deep, we find our fight,
A flicker shines, embracing night.
Through trials worn, our spirits grow,
Resilience blooms, with grace bestowed.

Like rivers flowing, fierce and bold,
We carve our paths, through lands untold.
With hearts aflame, we rise and soar,
From burdens borne, we learn to roar.

Each challenge faced, a lesson learned,
In every bruise, new strength is earned.
With open arms, we claim our place,
In struggle's grip, we find our grace.

From shattered dreams, we weave anew,
Creating light, our courage grew.
The tapestry of life unfolds,
In strain, we find our story told.

So let us march, with heads held high,
Embracing change, not asking why.
For in the dark, the seeds are sown,
From strain, our strength has truly grown.

Silent Rebirths

In quiet corners, whispers wake,
New life emerges, from what we break.
With every breath, a chance to start,
Transforming pain, into pure art.

The moonlight casts a gentle glow,
On tender roots, where hopes can grow.
A silent rebirth, in the still,
Unfolding dreams, a steadfast will.

With each soft step, the past recedes,
In tranquil hearts, a garden feeds.
We shed our fears, like autumn leaves,
In quiet moments, the spirit weaves.

Beneath the soil, a pulse, a beat,
Life's sacred rhythm, bittersweet.
Through silent storms, we learn to dance,
In every struggle, there's a chance.

So let the dawn break through the night,
With every star, a guiding light.
In stillness, hope begins to bloom,
As silent rebirths dispel the gloom.

The Garden of Renewal

In every heart, a garden grows,
With tender care, the promise shows.
From fractured soil, new life can rise,
Beneath the sun, the spirit flies.

With gentle rains, we wash away,
The remnants of a yesterday.
Let seedlings sprout, as we nurture,
In bloom, we find life's true adventure.

Each flower's hue, a tale retold,
In vibrant shades, our souls unfold.
With every petal, wisdom's gift,
In love's embrace, our hearts can lift.

Through seasons shifting, we renew,
In every storm, we learn what's true.
The garden thrives, with pain's release,
From ashes born, we seek our peace.

So sow your dreams, with open hands,
In fertile ground, where hope expands.
In unity, we find our strength,
The garden whispers, at great length.

Embers of Transformation

From ashes cold, the embers gleam,
In darkest night, we find our dream.
With faith ignited, the fire burns,
Through every twist, the heart still yearns.

Through trials faced, we forge our path,
In every storm, we learn to laugh.
With every spark, a new idea,
In transformation, we lose our fear.

Like phoenix rising from the flame,
We shed our past, yet keep the name.
In every struggle, wisdom's grace,
Embers flicker, lighting space.

From broken wings, we learn to fly,
In every tear, a new reply.
With courage bold, we claim our worth,
In embers bright, we find our birth.

So let the flames of change arise,
With every breath, we touch the skies.
Through transformation, we are free,
In embers of hope, we find our key.

Embracing the Echoes of Yesterday

In shadows deep, where memories dwell,
Whispers of time in silence tell.
Faces linger in the fading light,
Holding the warmth of love held tight.

A journey walked on cobbled streets,
Footprints left where heartbeats meet.
Fragments caught in a gentle breeze,
Bringing back moments with such ease.

Each laugh a note in a timeless song,
In the embrace of the past, we belong.
With every echo, a lesson learned,
In the flame of memory, brightly burned.

We gather the pieces, stitched up in care,
In the quilt of life, there's warmth to share.
Those whispers guide us through night and morn,
As we face the world, anew reborn.

Embracing echoes, we find our place,
In the tapestry of time and space.
With open arms, we greet the dawn,
For in the past, our dreams are drawn.

Reviving the Art of Connection

In a world where silence reigns,
We search for bonds in simple strains.
Eyes meet eyes, a spark ignites,
In whispered words, our hearts take flight.

A gentle touch, a knowing smile,
Bridges formed across each mile.
With laughter shared, we break the walls,
In this dance of life, the spirit calls.

Through screens and lines, we reach, we find,
The sacred threads that intertwine.
Reviving art that time obscured,
In connection's glow, our souls are cured.

We lift each other through shared breath,
In every moment, defying death.
Together we rise, together we fall,
In this tapestry, we are all.

From heart to heart, we weave the way,
Creating light where shadows play.
Reviving love with every chance,
In the art of connection, we dance.

Building Bridges of Hope

In the quiet, where sorrow lies,
A vision forms 'neath open skies.
Hands stretched forth, united we stand,
Together we forge, a hopeful land.

Constructing dreams with love and care,
Each beam a promise, strong and rare.
With every brick, a story told,
In colors rich, both brave and bold.

Through storms we travel, through winds that howl,
In laughter shared, our spirits growl.
For every tear that falls in vain,
We build a bridge in joy's refrain.

In the heart's embrace, we find our way,
Through trials faced, together we stay.
Building hope with every breath,
In unity, we conquer death.

With steadfast hands, we pave the road,
Lighting paths where love is sowed.
Building bridges, strong and wide,
In every heart, hope will abide.

Renewed Pulses of Affirmation

In the stillness, deep within,
A heartbeat echoes, soft and thin.
Each pulse a whisper of self-belief,
Bringing light to shadows, offering relief.

With every dawn, we rise, renewed,
In the dance of life, our spirits stewed.
Through trials faced, we claim our worth,
In every struggle, we find rebirth.

Voices lifted, strong and proud,
In affirmation, we stand unbowed.
Claiming space as we journey on,
Together we craft our vibrant song.

With grace we forge our paths anew,
In the warmth of friendship, hearts accrue.
Renewed pulses beating bright,
In the tapestry of day and night.

Each promise made, we hold so dear,
In the song of self, we find no fear.
With every step, we break the chains,
In renewed pulses, freedom reigns.

Love's Phoenix Rising

From ashes deep, a fire glows,
Awakening hearts where passion flows.
In shadows cast, new dreams take flight,
Love's phoenix rises, burning bright.

Through trials faced, we found our way,
In darkest nights, we chose to stay.
With every tear, a strength we gain,
Together soaring, free from pain.

Our hearts entwined, like vines they twist,
In the warmth of love, we coexist.
A journey long, yet never cold,
With every touch, a story told.

Through storms and gales, we stand as one,
Embracing light, outshining the sun.
No fear of loss, no doubt remains,
For love persists through all the pains.

As embers glow, our spirits rise,
In every glance, a sweet surprise.
Together forged, our fate entwined,
A love unbound, forever blind.

Tender Foundations of Tomorrow

In gentle hands, the future grows,
With whispers soft, the promise flows.
Each seed we plant, in hopeful ground,
A tender heart where dreams are found.

Through laughter shared and quiet sighs,
We build a world beneath the skies.
With every stroke of brush and pen,
We craft our lives, time and again.

A canvas holds our hopes so dear,
With every thread, we banish fear.
The bonds we weave, so strong and true,
Illuminate the path anew.

In moments made of simple grace,
We find the light in each embrace.
With every dawn, a chance to rise,
A tender love that never dies.

Together now, we take a stand,
With open hearts, we join our hands.
The future bright, horizons wide,
In tender dreams, we will abide.

Threads of Past and Present

In woven tales of days gone by,
We find the strength to reach the sky.
With every thread, a story spun,
Of love and loss, of battles won.

The past a guide, the present clear,
In every heartbeat, we hold dear.
Through trials faced, we learn to see,
The beauty found in you and me.

Each memory like a golden strand,
A tapestry that time has planned.
We gather threads with careful hands,
Creating futures, shared demands.

With every stitch, a promise made,
In colors bold, in light and shade.
Together weaving what will be,
A fabric rich in unity.

So let us bind our lives as one,
Through laughter shared and tears that run.
With threads of love, we'll stitch and mend,
The past and present, hand in hand.

Scattered Pieces

In broken shards, our stories lay,
A puzzle lost in disarray.
Yet in the cracks, old memories gleam,
Reflecting light, igniting dreams.

With gentle hands, we gather round,
To find the pieces that we found.
Through whispered thoughts and tender care,
A mosaic blooms, so rich and rare.

Each fragment speaks, a voice so bold,
Of hopes once bright, of tales retold.
In every gap, love starts to grow,
A garden wild, a vibrant show.

In unity, we shape our path,
Embracing joy, releasing wrath.
Though scattered wide, we still remain,
Connected hearts through joy and pain.

Together we'll transform the space,
With every piece, we find our place.
A tapestry of life we weave,
In scattered pieces, we believe.

Stronger Bonds

In every trial, we stand your ground,
A steadfast love, in you I found.
With hands held tight, we face the dawn,
Through thick and thin, our bonds are drawn.

Each challenge met, a chance to grow,
In unity, our hearts bestow.
Together built, the trust we share,
An anchor firm in troubled air.

Through storms that rage, and skies of gray,
Our spirits lift, we find the way.
With laughter bright, we light the night,
In every shadow, we hold tight.

So here we stand, with dreams aligned,
In every moment, love designed.
With open hearts, we pave the road,
A journey sweet, a shared abode.

In every sunrise, hope reborn,
Our stronger bonds, forever worn.
With every heartbeat, side by side,
In love's embrace, we shall abide.

Side by Side in Reclamation

Two hearts unite in the dawn's embrace,
Picking up pieces from a fractured place.
Together they rise, shedding old fears,
Hand in hand, through laughter and tears.

Each step a promise, every word a song,
In the garden of hope, where they both belong.
Building a future, brick by brick,
Side by side, a bond that feels thick.

Through storms they weather, through trials they tread,
Creating a story from love instead.
Roots intertwined, they flourish and grow,
In the soil of trust, their love will sow.

Together they dance, under starlit skies,
With dreams unfurling like fireflies.
In the quiet moments, their hearts align,
Side by side, their souls intertwine.

Reclaiming their paths with gentle grace,
In every heartbeat, they find their space.
Through the battles faced, they stand tall,
In the embrace of love, they conquer all.

Grains of Sand

Each grain a story, a tale to be told,
Whispers of time, both gentle and bold.
The shore stretches wide, the sea sings its song,
In the dance of the tides, we find where we belong.

Moments like grains, slipping through fingers,
The beauty of now, in the heart it lingers.
Each wave brings a promise, a future unfurled,
In the rhythm of nature, we find our world.

Sunset paints colors across the vast sky,
Echoes of laughter as the seagulls fly.
The sands shift beneath, yet remain ever true,
In the vastness of life, I find you.

Footprints together, then washed away,
Memories linger, though moments may stray.
In the ebb and flow, the journey's not done,
Grains of sand whisper, we are forever one.

So I gather these grains, with love I collect,
A treasure of moments, in hearts they connect.
On the shores of our lives, together we stand,
Crafting our dreams from grains of sand.

Future Castles

In the distance, dreams rise tall,
Brick by brick, we build it all.
With laughter and love, we sketch the plan,
Future castles, where we both can stand.

Imagination flies, like birds in the air,
Constructing a world, with strength and care.
Each room a promise, each stone a wish,
A sanctuary built from love's greatest dish.

Through passages wide, our hopes intertwine,
In this grand structure, our hearts align.
With every heartbeat, we lay the stone,
Building a home, a place of our own.

Windows to view the dreams yet to be,
In our future castle, wild and free.
Together we'll stand, through thick and through thin,
Where every new day is a chance to begin.

The towers will rise, touching the sky,
In this kingdom of love, we'll reach up high.
With laughter and warmth, we'll light up the night,
In future castles, our love shines bright.

Through the Pain, We Find Light

In shadows we wandered, lost and unclear,
Through the depths of sorrow, we clung to fear.
Yet in the twilight, a flicker began,
Through the pain we traveled, hand in hand.

Together we stumbled, but never alone,
In the hardest moments, our strength was shown.
Within every tear, a lesson was sown,
Through the pain we carried, our courage was grown.

The dawn broke softly, with hope's gentle breath,
From ashes we rose, defying the death.
In the warmth of new light, shadows recede,
Through the pain we found the strength to proceed.

With open hearts, we embraced the fight,
Knowing through darkness, we'll find our light.
Each trial a chapter, in our tale profound,
Through the pain we emerged, love all around.

In the tapestry woven with silver and gold,
We've learned in our journey, through warmth, not cold.
Together we rise, the past left behind,
Through the pain, we find light, intertwined.

Navigating the Waters of Renewal

In the stillness of morning, the waters await,
Glimmers of promise in every state.
With courage as compass, and heart as our guide,
We navigate waters where hope resides.

Each wave brings a lesson, each current a chance,
To embrace the unknown in this sacred dance.
We sail through the storms, though the skies may be grey,
Navigating the waters, we find our way.

With sails full of dreams, we ride the vast sea,
In the rhythm of life, we're finally free.
New horizons beckon, calling us near,
In the waters of renewal, we conquer our fear.

Together we journey, through depths we explore,
Horizon to horizon, our spirits will soar.
With every new dawn, we cherish the view,
Navigating waters, painting skies blue.

Let the waves whisper secrets of days yet to be,
In the ocean of life, there's magic to see.
As we chart our own course, side by side we'll thrive,
Navigating the waters, fully alive.

From Ashes

From ashes we rise, anew each day,
Embers whisper soft, guiding the way.
The past may be lost, but hope remains bright,
In the warmth of the glow, we find our light.

With every step taken, the ground feels alive,
In the heart of the fire, we learn to thrive.
Fragile yet strong, like a phoenix's flight,
We soar ever higher, into the night.

Through the smoke and the chaos, we find our path,
Learning from loss, facing the aftermath.
In the ruins we build, new stories unfold,
A tapestry rich, woven from gold.

Each scar tells a story, a lesson in grace,
The fires that burned, now a soft embrace.
With courage in hand, we reclaim our worth,
For in every ending, there's a rebirth.

So gather the ashes, let them ignite,
In the dance of the flames, find our own light.
For from the remains, new life will ascend,
From ashes we rise, on love we depend.

New Growth

In the silence of spring, new life awakens,
Fragile green shoots break through old foundations.
They stretch toward the sun with a gentle grace,
In the warmth of the earth, they find their place.

Roots dig deep, seeking waters below,
Nurtured by dreams, they begin to grow.
Leaves unfurl tender, reaching for skies,
In the dance of the breeze, a new hope flies.

Every petal that blooms is a story told,
In the colors of life, a vision bold.
With each passing moment, the garden unfolds,
A tapestry woven with joys and with holds.

Resilience shines bright in this cycle of time,
The whisper of promise in each gentle chime.
Nature's own rhythm, a harmonic thread,
In the symphony of life, love is our bed.

So cherish new growth as each season turns,
For in every ending, a lesson we learn.
From the roots of the past, we can rise and soar,
Finding strength in the soil, forevermore.

Songs of the Weathered Heart

In the chambers of time, where echoes reside,
A weathered heart sings, neither lost nor denied.
With notes of the past, woven deep in each beat,
A melody lingers, bittersweet.

Through storms that have come, with thunder and rain,
The heart has endured, embracing the pain.
Each scar tells a tale, of lessons and love,
As wings of the spirit soar high above.

In shadows and light, the song finds its way,
A hymnal of hope for each dawning day.
With whispers of courage, it dances and sways,
Reminding the soul of its vibrant arrays.

The rhythm of life carries whispers so true,
Of dreams that were cherished and paths that ensue.
With each passing moment, the chorus will swell,
In the heart's weathered song, forever we dwell.

So let us all listen to the heart's gentle call,
For in every note, there's a truth to enthrall.
Embrace the vibrations, let them all start,
For life is the symphony of the weathered heart.

Reconstructing Dreams

From fragments of hope, we piece it together,
Creating a future, no matter the weather.
With vision so clear, we map out the stars,
Transforming our setbacks into glowing memoirs.

Each dream that was lost comes alive once more,
In the echoes of courage, they begin to soar.
With hands held together, we build and we rise,
As the light of our passions ignites in our eyes.

The past may have shaped us, but we are not bound,
In the ruins of yesterday, new dreams are found.
With every small step, the tapestry grows,
In the garden of wishes, the future bestows.

Resilience is key, and belief is the spark,
In the canvas of life, we igniting the dark.
So let us create with the love we possess,
For in reconstructing dreams, we find our success.

Together we rise, like a phoenix from strife,
Building up new worlds, for this is our life.
With passion as fuel and courage our theme,
In the heart of the quest, we'll keep reconstructing dreams.

Harmony from Dissonance

In the chaos of life, we find our own tune,
A symphony rises beneath a cold moon.
With notes that collide, we search for the blend,
Creating the music our hearts can extend.

Strains of the dissonance vibrate with force,
Each conflict a chance to rediscover course.
As we learn to embrace all the jarring and pain,
We weave a new melody, joyful and plain.

The clashing of voices brings richness and depth,
In the chorus of life, we take every breath.
Together we rise, through the laughter and tears,
In unity's strength, we conquer our fears.

With every encounter, the harmony grows,
In the interplay, beauty uniquely flows.
Celebrating contrasts, we find common ground,
In the dance of the heart, love's language is found.

So let us create, with the dissonance near,
A tapestry vibrant, a music sincere.
In the art of connection, we find our own chance,
For harmony blossoms in life's grand expanse.

Unfolding from the Cracks

In shadows deep, a whisper stirs,
Life breaks free, as silence purrs.
From fissured earth, a tender shoot,
Emerges bright, with roots resolute.

Beneath the weight, resilience grows,
In darkest nights, the kindness glows.
With every crack, a story weaves,
Of strength and hope, the heart believes.

Embrace the light that spills from pain,
Through every storm, the soul will gain.
In breaking free, new worlds are found,
In fragile hands, the dreams abound.

From shattered pieces, beauty shines,
A testament to life's designs.
Each scar a badge, a tale unique,
Of courage found, and strength to speak.

So stand with grace, let flowers bloom,
From cracks of dark, dispel the gloom.
In every flaw, potential grows,
A symphony, the heart bestows.

Beyond the Edge of Grief

In silence deep, where shadows dwell,
A heart remembers, casts its spell.
Beyond the edge, where sorrow waits,
Hope flickers soft, as love creates.

As tears like rivers carve the ground,
In aching stillness, peace is found.
Each memory a sacred thread,
In woven hearts, the light is fed.

Through fog of loss, the spirit soars,
In whispered dreams, the heart restores.
Beyond the veil, where echoes play,
Sorrow holds hands with joy's ballet.

Embrace the night, release the pain,
For every storm will break in rain.
To mourn is love, to grieve is grace,
A journey that no time can erase.

In colors soft, the dawn shall rise,
Beneath the weight, a brighter guise.
For life, it bends but will not break,
In every heart, a love awake.

Rise of the Untamed Spirit

In raging winds, where wild hearts roam,
A spirit calls, and finds its home.
Untamed and fierce, in shadows cast,
A dance of dreams, both bold and vast.

With every breath, a fire ignites,
Through woven paths, the soul ignites.
In freedom's song, the heart will soar,
A journey blazed on ancient shores.

The tempest roars, yet calm prevails,
Through untamed lands, the spirit sails.
With roots that stretch and wings that glide,
In every storm, the heart will bide.

Embrace the chaos, let it be,
For wildness brings sweet clarity.
With open arms, let passions ride,
To rise again, with untamed pride.

Awake within, the heart shall rise,
To touch the stars, to claim the skies.
In every pulse, a truth shall reshuffle,
The spirit dances, fierce and supple.

Shattered Illusions

In fractured glass, reflections bend,
A world once clear, begins to end.
Each truth unveiled, each layer peeled,
In shadows deep, the heart is healed.

The masks we wear, they break apart,
Revealing depths within the heart.
In clarity, we find our grace,
As light erodes the hidden face.

Through shattered dreams, new visions bloom,
From ashes rise, dispel the gloom.
In brokenness, a strength ignites,
A mosaic formed of countless lights.

Embrace the flaws, they tell a tale,
Of journeys vast, where hearts prevail.
In every shard, a beauty's sewn,
From shattered illusions, love has grown.

So let them fall, the layers thin,
To find the truth that lies within.
A heart once lost can now be found,
In pieces scattered on the ground.

New Horizons

With dawn's first light, the world awakes,
A canvas bright, the heart remakes.
In every step, a chance to rise,
To paint the sky with vibrant ties.

Beyond the hills, where dreams take flight,
A journey calls, to hearts alight.
With open minds and spirits free,
We chase the stars, our destiny.

In sunlight's glow, we find our way,
Through paths unknown, come what may.
With every heartbeat, possibilities bloom,
In newfound hope, dispel the gloom.

So gather strength, and greet the day,
With joy and love, let fears give way.
In every breath, a chance to grow,
To find the light, and let it show.

As horizons stretch beyond the sun,
A world awaits, for everyone.
In unity, we forge ahead,
With open hearts, where dreams are fed.

The Dance of Recovery

In the stillness, hope ignites,
Steps of courage, soft and light.
Each heartbeat, a gentle sway,
Healing whispers guide the way.

Through the shadows, a spark will glow,
Finding strength in the ebb and flow.
With every stumble, we learn to rise,
Embracing the truth behind our cries.

The rhythm of time keeps us in tune,
Like flowers that bloom beneath the moon.
United we stand, never alone,
Together we dance, our courage grown.

With open hearts, we face the dawn,
In the dance of life, we are reborn.
Trusting the journey, come what may,
In the dance of recovery, we find our way.

Reimagined Connections

Threads of kindness weaving tight,
Bridging gaps with pure delight.
Hands reaching out, hearts intertwined,
In every gesture, love defined.

Old stories shared, new bonds take flight,
In laughter and tears, our spirits ignite.
Building bridges from pain to grace,
In every moment, a warm embrace.

Together we rise, our voices blend,
In a tapestry where hearts mend.
Celebrating each color, each line,
In the canvas of life, our souls align.

With every glance, a spark is born,
In reimagined connections, we are reborn.
Creating a world where love flows free,
In this dance of unity, you and me.

Mimicking the Willow's Resilience

Bending low, yet standing tall,
In each whisper, hear the call.
The willow sways in fierce winds' embrace,
Rooted strong in its sacred place.

Through storms and rains, it finds its grace,
A gentle dance, a calm embrace.
With branches long, it learns to bend,
In nature's rhythm, resilience trends.

Life's tempest may try to break,
Yet hope like leaves we shall not shake.
For every tear, a blossom blooms,
In the heart of struggle, joy resumes.

Let us mimic the willow's stance,
With every challenge, seize the chance.
To grow and thrive amidst the pain,
In life's wild dance, we shall remain.

Blossoms After the Storm

The grey clouds part, a gentle sigh,
Sunlight dances from a clear blue sky.
Petals unfold, soft as a dream,
After the tempest, hope's gentle beam.

Every droplet paints the earth,
In silence, we find rebirth.
With colors bright, the world ignites,
In blossoms' grace, we find our lights.

Whispers of spring in every grove,
Stories of resilience, a tale of love.
In the aftermath, we gather close,
With hearts ablaze, we raise a toast.

Together we bloom, hand in hand,
In the garden of life, we take a stand.
For every storm that passes by,
Brings forth the blossoms, reaching high.

The Art of Letting Go

In whispered winds, I find my peace,
A gentle nudge, a sweet release.
Memories fade like morning dew,
Embracing change, I start anew.

The weight of yesterdays must fade,
As scars transform, no longer spayed.
With open hands, I learn to trust,
In every loss, there's room for dust.

A feather's touch, the softest sigh,
In letting go, I learn to fly.
The heart expands, a boundless space,
To welcome joy, to find my grace.

Through each farewell, a new begin,
A story told, a freedom spun.
With every step, I choose my fate,
The art of letting go is great.

In golden dawns, I find my song,
In every right, there's been a wrong.
With every breath, I let it flow,
The beauty lies in letting go.

Mosaic of the Soul

Fragments of light, each piece a tale,
Colors collide, where dreams unveil.
In every crack, a story lies,
Each shard reflects our hidden skies.

From shadows cast, to brilliance found,
The soul's mosaic, tightly bound.
With every heartbeat, art unfolds,
In whispered truths, our essence molds.

Beneath the surface, layers weave,
In silent whispers, we believe.
Each hue a journey, each shape a quest,
In unity, our spirits rest.

Together we rise, a vibrant scene,
With open hearts, we dare to dream.
In every fracture, beauty glows,
The mosaic shines as love bestows.

With every breath, we craft our lore,
In the mosaic, we find our core.
Let rhythms pulse, let colors sway,
Our souls united in bright array.

Stitching Together Tomorrow

With thread of hope, I weave my dreams,
In every stitch, life's vibrant schemes.
Each patch a memory, sewn in time,
Together creating a life sublime.

Needles of purpose guide my hand,
As futures form where visions stand.
With colors bright, I craft the day,
In each connection, I find my way.

The fabric strong, yet soft and true,
Every tear mended, a tapestry new.
As moments gather, threads align,
In faith, I trust the grand design.

With joy and laughter, I patch the seams,
In every corner, the light redeems.
A quilt of life, both warm and wide,
Holding us close, a gentle guide.

Through needle's dance, the future glows,
In every stitch, the love still grows.
Together we build, together we mend,
Stitching tomorrow, hand in hand, my friend.

Luminescence After Darkness

When shadows fall, the stars take flight,
In depths of night, there brews the light.
With every trial, a spark ignites,
Illuminating the darkest nights.

In silence deep, hope stirs awake,
From ashes rise, new paths we make.
As dawn unfolds, the shadows flee,
A dance of light, setting us free.

Each tear that falls, a crystal bright,
Reflecting dreams, a future light.
Through every storm, we learn to rise,
With open hearts, we chase the skies.

Luminescence paints our souls aglow,
In the warmth of love, we learn to grow.
With every heartbeat, we find our way,
In darkness past, we greet the day.

A beacon shines from deep inside,
In unity, our fears subside.
Through battles fought and lessons learned,
We find our light, forever turned.

Milton Keynes UK
Ingram Content Group UK Ltd.
UKHW020815141124
451205UK00012B/585